NO DESTINATION

Poems by Tohm Bakelas

Kung Fu Treachery Press

Rancho Cucamonga, CA

Acknowledgments:

The author would like to thank the editors of these publications where some of these poems first appeared (in some form or another):

16 Pages, Algia Zine, Alien Buddha Press, Analog Submission Press, Beatnik Cowboy, The Beautiful Space, Between Shadows Press, Black Flowers Journal, Bold Monkey, Budget Press, Cajun Mutt Press, Cephalopress, Dumpster Fire Press, the Gasconade Review, Ghost City Press, Glove Zine, Holy&intoxicated Publications, Horror Sleaze Trash, Iron Lung Press, Mad Swirl, Medusa Publishing Press, Mythos Publishing, Outlaw Poetry, Origami Poems Project, Paper & Ink Zine, the Piker Press, Pyre Publishing, the Raw Art Review, Scriberlus, Scum Gentry, and the *Tower Journal.*

Table of Contents

"Most poetry is shit. But every so often, I'll find the perfect poem like the proverbial needle and I'll be hooked on that poet for life. As I find myself following their trail, seeking out any publication, chapbook, or collection they may have. For me Tohm is one of these poets. Over the years, I've got to know Tohm through drunken correspondences, publishing and of course when we've exchanged poems. This collection is a perfect starting point for anyone unfamiliar with Tohm's poetry and an essential edition for any Tohm Bakelas collection. These poems are raw, beautiful, grabbed from many fleeting moments, funny and sometimes tragic. Through psychiatric wards, barrooms and suburban New Jersey you'll see Tohm at his most vulnerable, strong and dangerous. These are perfect poems for a perfect collection."

– Gwil James Thomas: poet, novelist and inept musician.

"Tohm's words brim with life in all its extraordinary multitudes. It made me laugh out loud a great deal and provoked much thought. This is a very brave and beautiful book."

– Mark Anthony Pearce: poet

Decaying Sun Under Noontime Rain

Vacation Poems

No Place To Be

Cheap Booze and Shitty Poems

FOREWORD

Jason asked me to select some old poems and some new ones to package it into a book. There's a real trauma when looking back at previous work. There's also real embarrassment. I suppose that's just the way it goes though. In the three or four years since a lot of these poems were written and published I have developed my writing style, developed my skills, yet I still don't know what any of that means. But I'm trying.

I began writing poetry in March 2018 when the band's died. There was such an unreasonable pressure to write and publish that I often sent out unfinished ideas, littered with typos, and bizarre spacing and punctuation. I thought that the only way to make a name for yourself in the "scene" was to be heavily published—quantity vs quality.

Looking back, writing this now, I realize how wrong I was. However, it pays to understand where I was coming from.

Being in various New Jersey punk bands with no ambition other than to play anywhere and everywhere, never expecting pay, you are forced to survive as minimalists. What I mean is, we used to demo songs in our practice space before we hit the studio to produce the final recording. It was a way to get the raw ideas out without wasting time in the studio.

When I began writing poetry I applied the same principles of punk rock to poetry. In their original state, these poems that were originally collected in early and long out of print chapbooks, I view as demos. The way they appear here is their final recording. Unless you're a maniac and studied my work, you're not going to notice the changes. The integrity of these poems remains, but typos and spacing have been corrected. This is their final recording.

William Wantling, often in life, went through a similar phase as I face now, he'd write poems and submit them prematurely to magazines and publishers and then edit them later on in life when finally collected. I'm going through that now. My hope is that I have learned something from this process. I think I have.

I've titled this collection "No Destination." It seems as fitting as it is ironic, seeing as all these poems now have a home. Sometimes looking back isn't a bad thing.

Okay that's enough, I have to go now. Talk soon.

-Tohm Bakelas, October 2021.

For Dylan & Kaydence, friends, and MTS,
for everything.

its only one of the old doors

with its rusty hinges

swinging open for

a moment

in the universe

-d.a. levy

Orphan Crows

the moving amber

when my body
becomes
dust
and
dispenses
in the
wind
just know
i will
be back.

cool temperature

the rain hit the snow
with such force that
when the rain stopped
none remained

the fog became thick enough
you could taste it

the air smelled
like a decaying sea
salted and rusted out

the temperature
was cool and
refreshing

why can't
all days
of depression
feel as good
as this?

cherokee trail

when i was sixteen i used to visit her,
she was fifteen living in her alcoholic father's house

on damp nights of loneliness she'd call me over

i'd sneak through my grandparents' garage,
off the island, and down the road

she was never sober, always drunk or high on pills

she'd let me in, shushing me as she stumbled
up those unfinished, unstained wooden steps
that lead to her bedroom

and we'd lie down for hours and never talk,
we never fucked, being together seemed enough
and when she'd fall asleep i'd kiss her red hair
and say goodnight

one time when I left through the front door,
her father was outside waiting, cigarette in
one hand, beer in another, all he said was
"thank you"

i ran back to my grandparents' house
because i didn't understand then,
but twelve years later,
i understand.

words on walls

inside men's bathrooms
are carvings on stall walls
sometimes damning
sometimes humorous
sometimes insightful
i do not know if this world exists in
women's bathrooms
i have asked my wife
but she gives up no ghost
inside men's bathrooms
there is a jungle of lost poets
a true sanctuary for maniacs
armed with writing implements
scrawling their sacred paramount
words on walls
with no regret
with no remorse

orphan crows

orphan crows sit on a wire
as families attend church on sunday
and the homeless chase pigeons

orphan crows sit on a wire
as men change flat tires
and women sit powdering their faces

orphan crows sit on a wire
as gravediggers dig until the funeral begins
and return to finish the job when it ends

orphan crows sit on a wire
as two noontime lovers fuck
and the lonely think of suicide

orphan crows sit on a wire
as paramedics bring out an old woman
dead for a week in her recently paid off home

orphan crows sit on a wire
as cats howl in the street beneath
and dogs bark mad from inside homes

orphan crows sit on a wire
as the sun burns ripe tangerine
and the clouds explode white

orphan crows sit on a wire
as planes pass by overhead
some carrying passengers
some carrying freight
some carrying bombs

orphan crows sit on a wire
staring at a beautiful world
filled with human horrors
and human problems

orphan crows sit on a wire
stronger than the sphinx
more powerful than anubis
more final than the colosseum

orphan crows sit on a wire
as the tangerine sun sets
scattering streaks of purple
and red through the sky

orphan crows sit on a wire
as the sun continues sinking
and the sky becomes blackened and inky
like crow beaks and crow wings

orphan crows depart the wire
for the roost and the moonlight shows a vacancy
on the wire and the street below

and there is stillness as the moonlight
illuminates a sleeping landscape

it is peaceful
it is serene
it is lonely somehow.

Destroy My Wound

Summer 2010

we all got drunk together
in the basement of his parents' house
all of us had our hearts torn out within
a week of one another
camaraderie through heartbreak
drinking to feel less alone
each of us pondering internally what went wrong
no one dared explore these thoughts and feelings
it would have led down a narrow path of exacerbated
    drunkenness
when the night was over we stumbled to our cars
feeling no better
feeling no worse
some smoked cigarettes
no one talked
the stars offered no sympathy
and the moon was a cold slab of yellow fixed in the sky
eventually we had to go
we had work or school in the morning
some had both

for those few hours
drinking as homeless ghosts
it was the most alive we felt in years
and not much was spoken between any of us

overpriced beer

at a bar drinking alone
sitting in a lonely chair
staring at an empty booth
strangers everywhere
laughing and chatting
the froth fizzles and cracks
like embers from a dying fire
recollections of dead lovers
ghosts from past seasons
ghosts from yesterdays and yesteryears
time is but a pint
you drink from the top
and
then it's
gone.

school buses

in new jersey
maybe anywhere
people who
allow school buses
to enter
the flow
of traffic
deserve a special
kind of place
in hell

loneliness

loneliness is
no longer having a mother
gift you new socks on
christmas and your birthday
and having to do it yourself

loneliness is
walking through a parking lot
to the front entrance of your job
fighting back tears as the
wind repeatedly strikes you in the face

loneliness is
having a phone book
full of dead numbers
of people still living
who will never pick up

loneliness is
waking up at 4am as your children sleep
and your wife is in bed sleeping soundly
as you walk the cold floor
unsure of what to do

loneliness is
having a masters degree
and a career making a shit salary
that barely scrapes the bills
and further throws you into a pit of debt

loneliness is
having a brother in brooklyn
you never got to know
and have no idea how to get to know
and that's no ones fault but simply the way it is

loneliness is
having a father who works
harder than anyone you know
and has attained his dream of owning a diner twice
and continues to struggle in finding reliable help

loneliness is
having friends who you never see
more lonely than you
more mangled than you
who have pipe dreams they still chase

loneliness is
knowing your wife wants a divorce
but you want to try and fight it
shake off all the bad
attempt to start new
but don't know if she's checked out
and wonder why you choose to
mutilate yourself more and more
and more.

sometimes
loneliness is
not that bad,
but this time
it is that bad.

no more wishes

i want to find a field of dandelions
and soak them in gasoline
i want to incinerate them
i want to watch them burn
i want no one to make a wish
i want no more wishes
i want to take all the wishes
away from the world
i want to watch the dandelions burn.

want any eggs?

footsteps outside the door
handprints on the wall
what was here has been lost
long gone are the days of
slow dancing in the kitchen
and drinking beneath the stars
teardrops on faded floorboards
warm vessels dead and cold
hands barely touch never mind lips
words and thoughts foreign and lost
the threat of morning spawns sickness
kill the lights and stare into darkness
dancing with fireflies once brought
magic and comfort
no more blue skies
only violence and silence
eye contact is poisonous
a forgotten ritual of the past
streamlined isolation heightened and coexisting
walls and skin untouched by these calloused hands
your soft hands did all the damage
treason attempted on sacred vows
but the plans were caught and ruined
no apology was ever issued
this half-healed heart is wounded again
now,
what's in a house

but framed out rooms
with doors we slam
to shut each other
out.

tiny feathers

tiny feathers
from
unseen birds
caught
between
blades of grass
are
much like
black flies
trapped
in dew
soaked webs—
often
we
pass
by.

christmas carols

my coworkers angrily speak
of an occupant in the bathroom
who whistles christmas carols
every time he takes a piss.

my coworkers believe it's a man
based on the toilet seat always being up
after they enter the bathroom.

my coworkers hate this individual,
they call him an asshole, a real jerk,
a fucking lunatic, a sick bastard,
all for whistling christmas carols
every time he takes a piss.

they pound on the door
but he never emerges
he simply waits for it to pass
a true cool and calculated killer.

they still don't know who he is
or why he does what he does
or what pleasure he derives from
this behavior.

they don't know
that it is
me.

small victories

i came home from the hospital
and before i could even get out my car
she was waiting at the door,

she looked pissed and said
"there's fucking garbage everywhere."

i looked around and saw nothing.

she said "not out here, it's in the can. something
ate through all the bags, maybe a raccoon."

i took a look inside the can
sure enough the bags were shredded
and the garbage was fucking everywhere

"the garbage men will just have to pick up the
can and shake it into the truck," i said.

she stood there with her arms crossed
and let out this low "hmm," then
went inside and left the door open.

i thought to myself:
another day i have survived at work
another night i have just conquered at home.

destroy my wound

find the map
follow the paths
use a compass
navigate over mountains
cross old rivers
push through leaves
against the rain
against the sun
forward, onward
locate the cave
find the place
bring a lantern
swipe the cobwebs
remove the nails
take down the boards
scrape the moss
break the stones
chip away sediment
blow off dust
swat the flies
shoo the spiders
crack the layers
dig out ash
remove decay
sprinkle some water
peer inside
use the lantern
brush the dirt

sprinkle more water
cleanse the area
destroy my wound
feel the beat
rest your head
listen
close your eyes
let go
forget the clock
let go of time
chase the winds
follow the birds
hide from the sun
live under the moon
dance with fireflies
exchange songs with crickets
caress the willows
feed the crows
patch me up
bring me water
cleanse my soul
destroy my wound.

green river

i miss those days and
nights of driving around,
having no destination and
no place to go,
wandering and driving the
darkest corners of the earth
while listening to green river.

some nights we'd stay inside,
play cards and drink champagne
always while listening to green river.

i miss the magic of those times and find
any chance i can to put on that record,
drift to better times of slow dancing
on a moonlit kitchen floor,
embracing on a burning august night
as september winds passed by,
hoping that when i turned to my side
you'd be there.

if not this time
maybe the next time,
if not the next time
maybe soon.

when everyone asked me to
write a song
for them
you never did,
you never had to,
this one is for you.

In Living Rooms

Ashley Higgins

at $283 you listed your typewriter for sale
i low-balled you at $100
you came back at $150
i said no

a few days passed and you said your girlfriend
told you that $125 was a fair price

i agreed and drove to your house with Ben

you had three cats that we kept petting

you and your girlfriend asked us not to
but we were too stoned to stop

you demonstrated that all the keys worked
and you had extra ribbon which i happily accepted

i gave you the money and we left with the typewriter

later that night I sat down at the machine
a beautiful 1947 Royal Arrow C model

it was ready and i was ready

the lines were in my head

tap tap tap
tap

tap tap
click click

and that's when i saw it,
the ribbon wouldn't advance

i reached out to you asking for my money back
because clearly the machine didn't work,
i was very patient and very polite
but you said the sale was final

so here i am, down $125
with a busted typewriter
while you sit at home
with your three cats and girlfriend

i can't understand why
you had such a problem
with giving me my money back

you didn't have to be such a fuck about it

should this poem find its way to you,
i hope it makes you feel as uncomfortable
as you felt when we pet your cats
after you asked us not to.

George Dandusevki

dear george:

the typewriter works wonderfully
it is the machine gun
i have always dreamt of having
thank you for repairing
and breathing new life into it
death to the electric
long live the manual
the revolution and uprising
is coming george
be prepared

until the next time
your friend,
tohm

top ten feelings

i was home alone
when i discovered some
marijuana between broken
pens and torn pieces of paper
in a crowded drawer

i proceeded to get stoned
and naturally, the only
sensible thing to do,
was jerk off,
which i did

top ten feelings experienced:
eagerness, anxiety, bliss,
ecstasy, happiness, anger,
disgust, regret,
remorse,
and
shame

note upon the rejections

at first i didn't mind the rejections,
i was simply submitting poetry for fun,
but then it became addicting and
i couldn't stop writing,
sometimes one poem a day
sometimes two
sometimes six
and then i became mad with submitting,
the internet makes submitting easy,
i submitted 23 poems
to 14 different journals
in less than two hours,
but as the rejections came in
i started to hate,
i tried picturing these editors
sitting on their self-proclaimed thrones
callously tossing away poem after poem after poem,
i couldn't fix a face to a body
but i kept trying to see them,
kept trying to envision what slug was
setting fire to my submissions
stating, "while we appreciate the opportunity..."
when really
there is no appreciation
and
there is no opportunity.

something with poems

i sat down to write some poems
or submit some poems
or do something with poems
but i proceeded to smoke pot
and i got too high
and i ate cold ravioli lathered in garlic
and one cold fish stick left behind from dinner,
and then my wife came down stairs
because she heard the commotion
and she asked what was wrong with me,
but i just started laughing this uncontrollable laughter
and then she started yelling these
words that sounded so foreign
and i couldn't hear her anymore
because i couldn't stop laughing
and eventually she walked away
and then i found some paper
and i wrote this poem.

A Gathering of Grinches

This year
rather than a gathering of
Santa Clauses
I want to stage
a gathering
of Grinches.
The streets will run green
with Grinches
and Christmas will
never be the same again.
A good old Grinching
will take place.
A war between
Kris Kringles and Grinches
shall be waged.
The Grinches will rise!
Death to Saint Nicholas!
Long Live The Grinch!

Pop Culture

Dear Mr. Bakelas

"We were honored you submitted such interesting poems, however at this time we will be declining them as we are unsure how they entail Pop Culture. If you read the submission guidelines, all poems must follow the theme of pop culture. Your poems are quite morose and depressing and you write without punctuation. Please know we enjoyed the poems but they do not embody the theme of pop culture. Thank you for your time."

Sincerely,
The editors.

dear editors:

you are right, the theme of pop culture was
never present in my poems.
and please note this:
when i submitted the poems to you,
the holy editors,
i was completely numbed out of my skull,
in fact, i was so high, i remember thinking
this should be interesting
i know these poems will be rejected
but let me do it at the expense
of wasting someone else's time.
so holy editors,
sacred pompous editors,
of a sacred digital journal
thank you for writing this poem

sincerely,
t. bakelas

Decaying Sun Under Noontime Rain

morning crickets

morning crickets
are far more
fascinating
than
nighttime crickets

morning crickets
though minimal
and
less noisy
are
more deranged

they chirp on and on
as the warm sun
begins to cook
pink worms
on
hot concrete.

an aging son

my son will be 4 this August

he told me he didn't want to get bigger
he didn't want to be as big as me

i said "it's okay it's not that scary"
he said "yes it is" and looked away

i was thankful for that because
i understood too well,
i didn't want him to see my face,
i didn't want him to know

when he started to walk away
i gave him a hug and kissed his head

we went back to building legos
there was nothing else to do.

Bones Poet

a manic poet
with
manic stanzas
manic stories
and manic machinery
inside his leg.

he's got one eye
and the self proclaimed
Bipolar Frankenstein
had a heart attack
after christmas
and a second in april.

he went to urgent care
and flew first class in a helicopter
and was directly admitted into ICU.

after open-heart surgery
he was discharged
with instructions to wear a special vest
that monitored his heart rate
and instructions to remain
in bed.

"fuck that" he told me.

Bones Poet,
my friend,
he rides alone at midnight
and fishes alone in the sea.

A Message for Bones

after Bones
was discharged from
the intensive care unit
i called
to see
how he was
feeling
but he
didn't
pick up,
I left a message
wishing him well,
but that was a few days ago
and Bones never called back.
I guess
I'll
try calling
again
tomorrow.

reconsidered suicide

when you forget
about the lilacs
or the cardinal
or the dandelions
or the caterpillar
on silent blades of grass
something like a storm
can bring you back from that
and when you find yourself
feeling low and driving
headfirst into a storm
roll down the windows,
you are going to get wet
(that's inevitable and obvious
but you have a choice of just
how much)
and that's when you will feel it
that's when you will know
just how
good it
feels
to be
alive.

queen of the rosary

every noon she sits at the bar
fumbling her rosaries and
muttering incoherencies to herself
while sipping her vodka and beer

she only speaks to order another round

one day she was gone,
she never returned

i asked the bartender
what happened to her,
the queen of the rosary

he said he had no idea
what i was talking about
and gave me a beer

and that was that.

all the world is grey

when i think of blue
i think of the ocean,
not of loneliness
or sadness
or depression

when i think of those
three friends
i think of grey,
damp dark slate grey

and soon i feel grey

and all the birds in trees
and the sky look grey

and all the flowers in
suburban gardens look grey

and all the people i see look grey

and all the world is grey

two nights after

two nights after my fifth wedding anniversary
we went out to dinner at a new place because
our usual haunt was shut down

it was just us, no kids

my wife drank wine, i drank beer

sometime that evening i took a picture
of a glass of water with two floating ice cubes,
and in the background a flame flickered in the glass

we joked about death
mocked the waiters
and the laughter didn't die.

had it really been five years? where did it all go?

i didn't want the night to end but we had to go home

in walking back to the car, on the sidewalks
encompassing the green, i saw all the bums
smoking cigarettes, the former tenants of
my hospital, i felt like a king amongst the mad,
and they knew and i knew that this feeling
would disappear by tomorrow

i took the long way home to savor this magic

when we got home
i stood on the porch for some time

hai-ya

there was a moth
floundering on the hardwood floor
i spared its life thinking,
the light is almost gone,
but then my almost two year old daughter
ran up to it
stared and studied it
raised her foot
and smashed it
while yelling "hai-ya!"

we all laughed as she continued smashing

the massacre only stopped
after i picked her up

she gave me a high five
then punched me in the face
and yelled "hai-ya"

her brother was rolling on the floor
laughing uncontrollably

later that night
i slept with the lights on,

i was afraid i might be next.

pardon

"pardon?" she said

"another beer?" i said

she pointed to her glass which was
still very much full and smiled

i walked away, told the bartender "two beers"

when he delivered them i gave him the money
cranked one and tipped

he stared as i walked to the table with my other
beer

when i got there she said she needed a smoke,
she took my hand and weaved me through
a minefield of strangers, taking me away
from friends and away from my beer

when we got outside she stuck a lit cigarette
in my mouth and held my hand

i didn't understand

i kept thinking about my beer,
the one i left behind,
hoping no one would drink it

that thought was shattered
when she pulled me for a walk
and for the first time in a long time
i felt all right with the way things were

when i got back to the table
my beer was still there,
condensation and all

someone put
the ramones on the jukebox
the night was just getting started

on putting down a dog

when i got home
plates of food
remained
untouched
and left in place
as they had been before i left

every corner i turned
i thought i saw you
under blankets
and on the couch

every room i entered
i had hoped you would be there,
but you weren't

i couldn't allow you to
go on living that way

in your final act
you placed your head
in my lap and licked my hand

i kept petting your head
rubbing your ears
and then
it was over

thank you for being good to my kids
thank you for making this home special
i love you,
i'm sorry.

Vacation Poems

urge

sitting at the airport
waiting for the plane to arrive
i'm three and a half hours early

i watch people go by
strange faces go by
strangers go by

and i fight an urge to
stand up and shout:

"let it be known
i am feeling all right!"

however, this fought urge
is broken by a woman
smiling at me

i feel my cheeks redden
and i smile back

"excuse me, i'll give you $40
for your seat?"

an old man approached me,
$40 in hand and asked me
for my seat which had
extra leg room.

i said no to the money and
gave him the seat, i didn't mind.

he said he'd buy me a drink,
but he never did

however, this worked out anyway

my boarding pass granted me
free food and free booze

and now i'm two deep,
completely soaked in gin
feeling the turbulence
give me a hardon
and things couldn't be
anymore wonderful

killing off a feeling

i don't know how
it happened…
i was feeling
high off the gin
and the pressurized air
but i began reminiscing
the good times
and thought about
the finality
of the divorce
and i wanted
nothing
more
than to kiss her
the way
we used to
but tears
started pooling
and i immediately
killed that feeling
with another good hit
off the gin
and ginger ale.

waiting for fate

i chanced my
double gin
and ginger
against the
wonkiness
of the airplane
and marched down
the aisle
toward the back
of the plane
bashing
the shoulders
of strangers
while maintaining
the sanctity
of the drink

when i reached the bathroom
the stewardess said she could
hold my drink…

i wanted to ask her to hold
something else, but rather i politely
declined and went inside

while pissing
i drank the rest down
and emerged a titan

i asked for more gin and
was given two shooters

when i reached my seat
i carefully poured the sacred drink

i was fully erect waiting for
fate to fuck me or bless me,
caring neither way,
just happy things have been
this magical

a true story about flying first class

about SIX years go
the ONE and ONLY
time i flew
FIRST CLASS,
i went to the
GRAND CANYON
and DRANK the
ENTIRE
plane
OUT of rum
then
SWITCHED
to whiskey
feeling such
CHANGE
was a SUITABLE
substitute
but shortly
AFTER
the first whiskey
i passed out in the
BATHROOM
and my girlfriend
said they THREATENED
to GROUND the plane
if she couldn't GET me out
but ACCORDING to her
it was an EMPTY threat
and i AWOKE about
30 minutes BEFORE landing
and had no RECOLLECTION
of what happened

death defiance

the airplane light
to fasten
seatbelts
remains on
but my
seatbelt remains
unfastened

it's the closest
thing to death
in recent times
i've come by
and right now
it's all i've got

undelivered gratitude

on airplanes
i'm often
compelled
to walk to the
cockpit
and fling open
the door
and thank
the pilots
for flying me
to my
destination
but such
restrictions
are set in place
preventing me
from
doing so
and so i sit
in silence
and watch
the stewardess' ass
bounce
from one cheek
to the other
while
i consume
my free inflight
booze

he didn't seem to notice

i repeatedly
farted
in my seat
despite
sitting
next
to a
stranger

jerking off on a moving cruise ship

the boat was swaying from
side to side
and i gripped
the handicap bar
like it was my last chance
to feel alive

five days worth of
photographic memory
of young and old ass
in wet bikini bottoms
gripping tightly
exposing
clitoris and change

i closed my eyes and
opened the internal
photo album

i began
cranking away
while the sea
carried
me home
and finished
me off.

five hours before the flight home

i hadn't thought about work once
this entire vacation except on the final day

sitting in the airport watching
strangers pass by and seeing
a select few responding to
internal stimuli and communicating
with unseen forces and interacting
with delusions that only they could see

and i smiled seeing these individuals
carrying on, pushing forward,
knowing that in two days i'd be
back at the hospital running groups,
getting spit on, dodging punches,
and receiving death threats

and no matter how
terrible the future looks
i still look forward to
the setting sun,
the rising moon,
and the New Jersey
nighttime air

a weak stomach cured by inflight pretzels

flying on a
weak stomach
cured by
inflight pretzels—
serving size one,
calorie count eighty—
my stomach is now iron.

the stewardess that comes by
has red hair and an accent
i can't quite place.

her face shows the years of flying
and dealing with people like me,
and before she departs i order
two gins and one ginger ale.

i'm ready to feel the
defiance of gravity
beneath my shoes
at an altitude of
twenty nine thousand
and three hundred feet.

"it's complimentary, man"

the guy
sitting next to me
is double my size
in height and weight
and after i ordered
two gins and a ginger
he ordered a jack and coke
and attempted to pull out a credit card
but i stopped him and said
"it's complimentary, man"
he replied
"as it should be
putting three big guys
in the same
row of seats"
i laughed an honest laugh
and pounded
my drink,
there was
nothing more i could do.

complimentary drinks are meant
to be drank

smiling, my soon to be ex-wife jokingly asks,
"do you need gin on every flight?"

the stewardess stares as i quickly answer

"it's complimentary... yes"

two delivered and two drank

she's asleep and i run
to the back of the plane
for more

from row 8 i watch on

often i fantasize about the possibility
of dating an airplane stewardess
and find romance in the distance apart

she would travel the country or the world,
while i work monday through friday at the hospital,
and return to the house i grew up in,
while visiting my children in the house
i still own with my soon to be ex-wife

and every night the stewardess would phone me
from another city, another state, another country
and we would talk about our days
and speak of the lonely times
apart from one another

but i haven't the guts nor the paper
to deliver my sentiments
to any one of these beautiful women
on this particular flight

one stewardess resembles
the girl i took to prom,
just older and aged,
and i wish to say hello

but she only serves first class
and i'm stuck
in coach.

afterwards i made the mistake
of talking to her

the stewardess
i fell in love with
pulls the grey lace
curtain back
segregating first class
from the rest of us

her smile is soft and
eyes are pale brown
and i watch as she
gives a thumbs up
to one passenger
and winks at another

i'd give anything to be
either one of them,
just to embrace
those gestures,
faked or genuine

internal resumé

the pressure
in this plane
sounds like i'm
driving through
a two mile
single-lane tunnel
at one hundred
miles per hour
with all four
windows down

nothing but space and time
can disturb this turbulence

except a new problem
has presented itself

i drank the entire plane out of gin
and the effects of such vacancy are
much more debilitating
than the combined effects
of intoxication and
altitude poisoning

however i add this to
my internal resume
of consuming free
inflight booze
and conquering
all free drinks.

the plane is spinning and no one notices

the first class
stewardess
walks by,
smiles
at my
sleeping son
and ignores me

i feel the plane
spinning in circles
and know we are
going to be all right

the remaining gin is dwindling

the guy next to me twirls his
jack daniels bottle in his fingers,
it keeps him grounded

i float above
without a world
to feel at home

i impatiently wait
for a stewardess
to walk by with
an undiscovered gin
while i sweat in my seat
and await landing.

No Place To Be

the streetwalker in my neighborhood

everyday i see him out there
walking along the roads
he has the posture of an emu
and the grace of a gazelle
he carries a radio
that only he can hear
it screams static
and nothing else
all the neighborhood dogs
bark at his presence
sending him running to the
opposite side of the street
he stops and speaks to
water drains and sewer lids
and always follows the same steps
maintaining his routine
completing his ritual
guided by unseen forces
that will never be understood
by the common man

everyday he walks along the roads
knowing where the sidewalks end
and appearing content
in never knowing
where a new adventure begins

there he goes again

there he goes again
running down the street
faster than ever
his radio is loud today
i can almost make it out
it kind of sounds like johnny thunders,
or the stooges, or even the germs…
now he's no longer running
he's standing on the sewer lid
and green sparks are shooting
from his eyes and mouth…
i turn away from the window
and pace through the house
searching for my ex-wife and kids
but no one is home…
i return to the window
and see his entire head
submerged in the water drain
and from beneath the street
turquoise light has enveloped him
and his body is floating in the air…
i leave the window
find my shoes
put them on
unlock the front door
and get outside…
but when i arrive he is gone
and the turquoise light

and green sparks are gone
i walk across the street
to the sewer lid
and kick it with my foot
i walk to the water drain
and peer inside
nothing is down there
no one is there…
my neighbor comes outside
and asks if i'm okay
i don't respond…
under a creamy violet sky
i quickly walk back to my house
get inside
and lock the door,
what else could i do?

served time

by the way he walks
i can tell he served time
shuffling his feet
barely lifting them
from the ground
like he's shackled
to invisible chains

outside the grocery store
he collects shopping carts
with his impaired gait
never complaining
completing his job as required
only speaking to coworkers
all of whom he calls "boss"

every day i drive to that store
park my car and go inside
get lunch from the salad bar—
typically a fresh scoop of tuna
covered in three bean salad
occasionally coupled with a soda
but usually a bottle of water

and after i pay i see him out there
lethargically dragging his feet
robotically collecting the carts
although we've never spoken
i know he's served time
though in which hospital
i do not know

two different shifts

the prison inmates
walk the hospital parking lot
cleaning up trash
and cigarette butts
that didn't make it into the can
they make the best of the day
laughing and joking
working their shift
with true camaraderie
these trash collectors
say hello to no one
they serve their time
under the rising sun
wearing bright orange prison regalia
and every morning they are here
pacing the parking lot
while i sit in my car
comfortably watching
as i wait
for my own
shift
to begin.

trees dance

all the trees
outside my window
look like people
with outstretched arms
begging for forgiveness
from unseen gods.
white and green moss
grows on the bark
disfiguring these trees
making them
ugly yet beautiful
imperfect yet not untouchable.
these trees instill a comfort
that most people cannot
and in the wind
they dance
and will outlive
you and me.

a clean but filthy, poorly-lighted place

i like the chaos of the place
the music is louder than need be
tortured women slurring words
swinging breasts, hip, and ass
under glowing red lights
the place is dark
remarkably clean but filthy too
i find it all right
the women dance
the beer is served
i write the poems.

nervous tic

i peel the label
off my beer
as a nervous
tic
and paste it to
the bar countertop
as i study
the skin of
the blonde next to me—
it is dry and cracked
with faded freckles—
i think about telling her
the name of some
good moisturizers
i don't
i abandon it
i do not belong here
i do not wish to exist
but the night is still young
and i've got no place to be
so i'll sit for a while
and maybe the luck
will arrive
and besides
just sitting here

i've already made
some people uncomfortable
and written three poems
this being
one of
them

the suicide of katelyn davis

the sun sets into darkness
as unfamiliar cars drive by
and neighborhood dogs bark at nothing
an apparition dressed in child's clothes
dangles from a tree like a wounded fruit
inside homes families are preparing dinner
the phone keeps ringing without an answer
as the twilight settles
the silhouette dances in the wind

porch swing

it was 2:30pm when i got there
she sat on her mother's porch
smoking a cigarette
she had been awake since 9am
and started drinking vodka around 11am
she told me she needed help
finding a screw or a nail
to hang something on the wall
the smell of vodka on her breath
turned me on
something about vodka and beer
on a woman's breath
does that
she wasn't wearing any makeup
i said she looked pretty
she told me she cried it all off
the night before
when we couldn't find a nail
i sat with her
rocking back-and-forth
in a swing that
hung from the porch ceiling
when she stopped smoking
she wrapped her arms around me
there was no more talking
the creaking chair spoke loud enough
this continued on for some time
after i left

she found a nail
and hung her painting on the wall
on the drive home
i thought
sometimes we need that
sometimes we need to simply be
we need quiet afternoons
with someone
even if no words are shared
sometimes it's what
keeps us
from suicide
or worse
sometimes it's what
leads us
there.

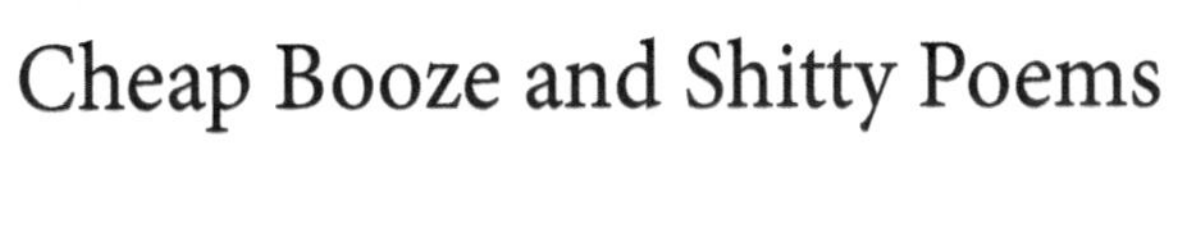

Cheap Booze and Shitty Poems

an observant bartender

she asked, "you write poems?"
to which i replied, "sometimes i do"

she laughed a laugh
that would cut
an ordinary man down
but i was unaffected
by her attempt
to scathe me

she asked, "what are your poems about?"
to which i answered,
"the crusade to end all humanity"

she shifted in her seat
and looked around the bar
scanning all the exits
i said nothing more
and soon she left

the bartender asked, "what happened?"

i didn't answer
i drank my beer
under the glow of dying light

the perfect set up for a shitty poem

it was the perfect set up
five customers
the bartender
and me.
there was no catalyst for interruptions
and the music was low.
under such circumstances
it was the perfect set up
to write some poems
and drift casually
and methodically
into the reigns of
inebriation.
i took my seat
in my usual corner.
the bartender
placed the beer before me
and i began to write.
after the first good hit of the beer
my plan was shattered immediately.
the inside of the bar
began to smell
like the outside
of a sewage plant.
the beer tasted good
fresh, crisp, and no suds
but the smell of
the bar

alone
kept me sober.
everyone around
me kept drinking
as if nothing was wrong
as if the smell of shit
didn't permeate
in the hot july air.
i quickly began
drinking
as a means to
destroy my
olfactory senses
and render my mind useless.
a futile attempt at
forgetting the smell
and writing the poems.
it didn't work.
i couldn't write anything.
i couldn't finish anything.
the only thing i could do
was drink more
and write this shitty poem.

The Day I Met Bones

he said his name was Bones,
and that he wrote poetry and
slamdanced to the Ramones.
and as he articulated
his life's past
i listened to every syllable
and tried to keep up with his
tangential ramblings
but eventually
the overstimulation
of his mind and tongue
declared a peace treaty
and he abruptly
stopped his stories
only to say
"thanks for listening, when's lunch?"

a nice way to end a day

she asked, "do you like
working at the hospital?"

i said, "i do"

she asked, "do you see
anything bigger or
better for yourself?"

i said, "there's absolutely
no need, i'm happy here"
and then i asked her
the same

she said, "i have two more
years to retire and at
62 years old i hope to retire
and find a boyfriend"

i told her i didn't believe she
was actually 62 years old,
maybe 42 but not 62

she said "believe it or not, these
used to be double d's"

i smiled and said "isn't that something?"

she said, "they're now c-cups"

i said, "well maybe next time i'll take a look"

she laughed, grabbed my right arm,
and squeezed hard

we walked
in silence together
for a bit
and then she went back
to her desk
and i went home

Under The Same Moon

on scene

it was sunday may 6th,
we met up at the cemetery
where my grandparents reside
to bury a portion of
what remained of my mom.
it had been five months
and two days
since she died.
we stood around
not saying much,
amazed we even found the gravestone.
i learned i was the only one who
still visited the cemetery,
it was strange after that.
my dad asked if we wanted to eat somewhere,
everyone said yes,
i said no.
my children were at home and waiting for me.
they wanted to come to this experience
but i wasn't ready to explain
how a woman they once loved
was stuck in an oven and reduced to ash,
it was heavy enough
explaining death to a 3 year old.
eventually i departed the others
and when driving home became
emotional and then angry,

it began to rain which was rather nice
but there was too much traffic
prohibiting any flow of moving cars.
i saw a small window of opportunity and
went for it.
in the process
i scraped the side of a white truck
and the back of a black car.
not needing any more shit
i jammed the gas pedal to the floor and took off.
in the chaos i somehow landed
on an exit ramp from a highway
and as cars were approaching
i quickly maneuvered a k-turn
and drove straight through the red light
where the dust was still settling
from the chaos i had created.
on scene
there were people bewildered
on their phones calling police,
calling loved ones,
calling priests,
calling god.
i kept driving and got out of there.
i took a turn down a side road
and found a different highway.
when i got home
i scraped the paint off my car
and ran inside.
i shut all the windows,

closed all the curtains,
and turned off all the lights.
i waited for it all to pass
or catch up to me,
there was nothing more i could do.

firefly field

on holy nights
on lonely nights
we'd gather
in a drunken haze
at the field behind
the parking lot
across from the hospital—
there were hundreds of fireflies
lighting up the night,
creating magic,
providing sanctity—
often we'd walk around
that field or sit in silence
and watch
as the night came to life,
and then we'd go
home,
back
to our
own
hells.

stagnant puddles

as children we expect our mothers and
our fathers to live forever
we envision them immortal and
we challenge their ways
then death comes and
picks off one grandparent at a time
an uncle suicides
a divorce is finalized
and the puddles we once jumped in
remain stagnant and lonesome.

the bogeyman we once feared
becomes credit card debt
student loans
rent or a mortgage
car payments
a hospital bill
the electric bill
the gas bill
it is endless and it has always been,
but as children
our parents shielded us from
this shit.

some days there is a harmony
like old chimes blowing in the wind,
though no chimes are outside

and no wind is present.
i do not know what this means
but it continues on
and this harmony
brings about a forgotten peace
that was once found in those
now stagnant puddles.

baptismal blast

the bartender
spilled
beer all over
my right
arm
then ran over
and dabbed off
the liquid
while endlessly apologizing.
"forget it" i said "it's all right."
she said "it looks like
we're both
having the
same
sunday."
i smiled
then quickly
and uncomfortably
took a deep hit—
i felt the years
slide down my throat,
all the abuse i've
dished out
to bartenders here,
all the fucked up threats
i've loudly unleashed
in vain of having fun,
but in her eyes
i found forgiveness

i found empathy
and the spilled beer
was a baptismal blast
from that unseen god
i lost the number of—
i drained the glass
and wrote this poem.
a few moments later
i attempted to read the words
but discovered complexity
and confusion in the content.
not wanting this challenge
i slapped the countertop
and shouted "alright! give me another!"

beneath a black rim hat

my
eyes
stare
at the
man's
eyes
from across
the bar—
bags upon bags
droop down below his sunken dark eyes—
he buries his face beneath a black rim hat,
buries his face right into the glass.
he and i,
we share the same woes,
but i've never
stuck a needle in my arm
hoping for more.
i only look away
when he gazes
into my eyes
searching for secrets
but my eyes
share none.

closure

the flags are
raised
full-staff
and the crow's nest
is on
fire
the altar servers
are drunk on
holy blood
and the street preachers are
involuntarily committed

i watched him
jump
from the
fourth floor window
and hit concrete
covered in rock salt
and geese shit
while i ate tuna salad
and scratched
my belly.

worthwhile

the corner bar seat
provides
endless views
of the barmaid's ass,
opportunities
to fill the draft
with her assistance and
without her knowledge,
and convenience
to write the poems.
the corner bar seat
is a lonely place
but i do not
feel
alone.
the barmaid
keeps looking back,
is it towards the draining glass
or my ugly unsettling self,
the barmaid's smile
is natural and warm
making things
seem okay for now,
making this seat
worthwhile.

Li Po

Li Po fell from his boat
in drunken glory while
attempting to embrace
the reflection of the moon
in the Yangtze River

down down he went,
taking all the wine
and his blazing poems
down with him

Li Po, centuries later,
your words from the
Tang Dynasty
rip me apart

tonight when I see the moon,
I think of you

and should we meet in the Star River
bring your wine, I'll bring my beer,
we will toast humanity
from New Jersey
to China

Li Po,
see you
soon.

New Poems

two cold beers riding shotgun

i drove all day in a haze,
there was fog in my head
and my eyelids were heavy.
i didn't care where the road went
if i crashed or arrived
i had no destination
the car drove me…
from town to town
from paved rock to dirt
from day to night
my fog never lessened,
it was too real.
it followed
under highway lights
and beneath overpasses
and all the small town
street lamps that i passed
remained off—
i wondered who controlled them…
eventually, my fog subsided
when i reached
another town,
another hell.
two cold beers
riding shotgun.
i drank them down navigating
Frost's lost roads…

when the car stopped
i was free
and the stars
belonged
to
none.

the humble duster

down in laredo
at the intersection of
san bernardo ave and interstate 35
he stands draped in his black duster
like an old wooden cigar store indian

it was 103 degrees when we saw him out there,
dry blazing heat, no humidity, no breeze

some say he is a homeless tweaker
cooked out on meth,
some say he is an arsonist
who burned his family to ash
and fled to laredo for a new life,
others say he's not even there at all.

but i have seen him
standing there in laredo,
at the intersection of
san bernardo ave and interstate 35

standing as the sun sets on the city under seven flags.

in case anyone wanted to know
what i did with the hair that falls out
during the shower...

i leave it there
hopeful
that it will grow
into something magnificent.
hopeful
that it will learn
how to cook for me,
read to me,
wipe my ass for me,
dust the furniture,
clean the litter box,
balance my checkbook.
and someday
i can teach it
how to be
an amazing creature,
far better
than the human
that i ever could be
and ever would be.
so don't be
alarmed
if you
see it
there,
staring at you,
just nod a hello and move on.

the importance of solitude

you got a lot of nerve…
and another thing,
you know you fucked with me,
i know how you operate…
you love to tell me
about all the women
you've fucked
but you've never fucked me!
you still haven't
fucked me!
and you tell me
about all the women
who have hurt
you from your past,
yet you still talk to them…
you even talked
to one
tonight!
i watched you talk to her!
and i don't tell you shit
because i don't need you
feeling some type of way…
you know what you intend to do,
don't even try to say otherwise…
you got a
lotta nerve…
anyway
i love you,
goodnight.

revolution in a carpet shop

my friend invited me to an open mic night
that was taking place in a carpet shop
and for some time i debated on staying home.

i decided to attend because
my walls were no longer friendly
and i figured a change of scenery
might be beneficial for my health.

when i arrived i was completely stoned,
and as a means to avoid sitting in close proximity
to anyone and everything i didn't know,
i began rearranging the rows of chairs lined
beneath all the carpets hanging overhead

i stopped because there was
an influx of tie dye shirts,
body odor, and dreadlocks,
all of which was heightened
by my higher sense of awareness

i began to panic, but that was broken
when my friend played sonic reducer
on his acoustic guitar

as soon as he finished
a guy wearing a tie dye shirt stood up

and started shouting revolution:
that he was tired of being suppressed
and that we as a community needed to unite
and grow an organic garden for all
the people of the town as a means of sustaining
everyone and everything because soon
the entire world would starve
and people would begin killing one another
and ultimately it was us versus them

when he stopped
he looked out towards
those in attendance
and many people
stood and clapped

i sat there laughing and that's when it began

i felt the rumble beneath my feet
as the chairs around me started sliding away

i continued laughing as the parting of chairs
provided me an exit and much like moses
i walked on through

outside my friend gave me a cigarette
the guy who spoke of revolution
came over and asked
what was so funny about his speech

not wanting to
further crush
his revolution
i shook my friend's hand
and went home.

invisible suffocation

it happened again. i don't know how it found me
this time, but someone must have sold me out.
i was alone in medical records, reading a former
patient's chart when i felt it. i couldn't avoid it. i ran
from the room with my papers clutched in my hand
like a crucifix until i reached an unfamiliar ward on
the second floor, but it was there too. it kept hunting
and following me. and on the third floor i was
walking with patients, but it found them too. they
began screaming and instructed me to flee. i managed
to get into the staircase where i leapt down two flights
of stairs before making it to my desk. but when i got
there, it was sitting in my chair, calmly waiting. and so
i submitted to it. and on lunch break it rode as my
passenger, my copilot on this journey in hell, its claws
clasped between my ribs, with strength that
manifested from all the years of sadness from this
hospital. my watch offered no escape. 4 o'clock was
three and a half hours away. that's a long time to wait
in a sadness that is not yours.

seagulls circle the sky

an empty clear ziploc bag
sits in the parking lot
crumpled and discolored
containing vacant space—
uninterested in its existence
wind passes over
leaving the bag behind—
i pass by
wondering
what the bag
contained

route 10 reflection

as i drive in silence
with the windows rolled down
jerry's kids plays on inside my head.

beneath my tires
the concrete screams
and all the traffic lights are green.

having no destination, i continue to drive,
i'm between two homes, a pending divorce,
and awaiting new furniture.

i didn't do much today, i hadn't
thought about much today.

jerry's kids ends, negative approach now plays.

no one is out on this street tonight,
and it's beginning to rain

the ashes of yesterday
are pressed into
the diamond of today,
it's a shit cut and the
clarity remains
to be seen.

burning cigarette in february cold

i always
liked the way
street lights
shined off
the rainy road
and the way
a lit cigarette
exploded
from a moving car
onto the still blacktop
shooting orange sparks
into
an ever-changing
world
i reminisce
these images
as i roll
a burning cigarette
between
my fingers
feeling
the fire
getting
closer

trying to focus on the hockey game

so much ass flab
and poorly implanted tits
shaking in my direction
shaking in my face
i tell the whores to fuck off
i tell them i'm not interested
only one complies and wanders off
she returns with wine for herself
and a beer for me
"i didn't pay for that"
she says nothing
smiles and
takes the seat
next to me
we watch the game together
occasionally she places
her hand on my
right leg
i let it slide
it keeps her grounded
in this reality
and it does the
same for me too.

masturbating with a headache

the moonlight
shines off the snow
and into my home
illuminating the perimeter
of the dark room.
outside the rustling leaves
sound like chains being dragged
by giants
crunching snow
under glass boots
handcrafted by cthulhu
himself.
something scales
the exterior wall
scaring the cat
whose imagination
is obtuse
but more existent
than many
i know.

jerking off with a stomach virus

after i vomited all over myself twice
and the bathroom floor three times
and after i shit so many times i lost count after 19—
however later skimming through text messages
sent to friends during a period
i thought i was dying
leads me to believe it's closer to 26—
twelve hours later,
after all that,
i was feeling better,
good enough to jerk off
and believing this was the way to enlightenment
i nearly passed out finishing the act
and when the room stopped spinning
and i regained strength
i cleaned up
all the wasted semen
on my belly,
another unborn child,
another unborn life,
and soon afterwards
i wrote this poem
then fell asleep.

king of the mad

sifting through madness
one thread at a time
i work with patients,
the maddest of the mad,
hospitalized since 1968 to now—
every year in between
and every year after—
these lifers
these chronics
they remained hospitalized
through deinstitutionalization
and watched as others
were released
these patients are the reason
this hospital exists
and as i walk amongst them
i feel safe here
i am king of the mad
these patients don't understand
credit cards
cell phones
or computers
they don't know about
brita filters or self-check out
and i fight
every day
to keep them inside
this is their home
this is all they know

an extra security measure

black ants
march the
dark part
of my mind
as cicada wings
beat in the
tangerine spring
and deer drift
my greening lawn

my neighbor
next door
has an
airbnb
and
because of
this
i lock the
front door

thank you

it's these damp wet new jersey nights
when i pace the cold floorboards alone
hearing the rain bounce off the windowsill
that i think about the nights of
walking you
through the house
into sleep
while your little eyes
watched me closely in the darkness
as i sang you my redemption songs
with guitar intros hummed to death…

nervous breakdown, sonic reducer,
j. thunders, rain dogs, minor threat,
nebraska, and so much more…

it's those nights
walking in the moonlight
past curtain-closed windows
with you both in my arms
singing these rebel lullabies
while you closed your little eyes
and let out tiny gentle snores
that i felt
just how
truly beautiful
life could be…
dylan and kaydence,
i love you.

it's not your fault

i grind my toes into the carpeted floor
thinking about the names of all the liquors
we drank in those early days
and recall all the tastes and smells
that accompanied those drunken nights.

and it's not your fault
i grind my toes into the carpeted floor
knowing that those days and nights
are long gone and will never return
but when we spend time together,
sometimes i get confused.

and it's not your fault, but mine.
because somewhere deep down i think i
once believed that things could have gotten better,
and somewhere deep down i think i
might have believed that not all was lost,
and somewhere deep down i think i
may have believed in us.

but i now know it's misplaced
and unfounded
and a lost cause.

and just like rocks
placed on gravestones
the dead remain
dead but
i keep
living.

cradle worms and ants

sometimes i see a specter
a glimmer of someone i feel i know
a ghost of someone i feel like i could know
but it falls under the haze of dim lights

so i stare outside
through a dirty glass window
and i see an oily cloudy night sky
and i think about all the crooked spines
that i've walked and kissed
but it's a futile attempt
at distraction from listening
to conversations around me
conversations that are uninteresting

and so i trace the lines
in the palm of my hand
wondering if they'll
ever be traced by
foreign fingers again
almost hoping rather
that they can cradle
worms and ants instead
knowing that they are
harmless and
want
nothing
in
return

airplane poem

seeing civilization like ants
and buildings like cardboard boxes
makes me cherish
moments of disappointment
and letdowns
and heartbreak
and magic of real romance
and feelings of significance
because through it all
one way or another
a gravestone is involved
or depending on the stomach
a wake or a funeral

and lonely nights at bars
filled with exes
and failed attempts
of moonlit slow dances
brings more hopeful prospects
than the current situation

because even
a broken compass
leads to
worthwhile
explorations
sometimes
you just
have to wait

dentistry and the electric chair

though a lousy dentist
alfred p. southwick
is credited
as the inventor
of the electric chair

on august 7 1881
he witnessed
a drunken dockworker
grab a live generator terminal
and instantly die

a day shy of exactly 9 years
on august 6 1890
william kemmler was executed
by the electric chair
in auburn prison in new york

southwick was present
smiling with a hard-on
as his invention
worked as
he had intended

now every time i get
my teeth cleaned
i wonder if my dentist
will throw the switch
that will do me in.

a poet wants specific examples

i went to a poetry reading
and liked what i was hearing
so i waited until the end
before saying to the reader,
"i enjoyed what you wrote."

they asked, "what did you enjoy?"
and then asked for
specific lines as examples.

when i couldn't do so
they scoffed
and muttered
something insolent
and suggested
i take notes
next time.

at the next reading
i remained silent
afterwards.

and after that reading
i never
went
back.

the dead come alive in my room
at night when i'm alone

empty quiet nights
used to bring joy
listening to
chattering crickets sing
chattering-cricket songs
while autumn breezes
gently kissed faces of loneliness.

and under cloudless evenings
a wholesome moon
that was the only visitor
ever worth greeting.

but now these empty quiet nights
bring about stagnant silence
and acceptance of the dark.

there is nothing more.

dark black rain

i wait in dark black rain
in the heat of night
for your dagger stares
and knifing touch
only to be let down
by the human possibilities
of manipulation
intoxication
miscommunication
and misinterpretation…
this once promising evening
turns into a public hanging
and the invisible noose
tightens around my throat…
the heat of night turns cold
as i wait in dark black rain

PO Box 394

sometimes i get lucky—
i have days
where i can
drive around
with the radio off,
the music off,
my thoughts off,
my mind off—
and i find myself
parked
in front of the
post office,

and the ritual begins:
fumbling through
junk to find
the key to my
po box,
then going
inside to
open it.

most usually,
this 3x5 box
contains
month old
coupons, shopping ads,

surveys about which
political party i belong
to, and mental health
resources.

but every once
in a while i
receive poems, art
books, photographs,
from people all over the world,
mostly writers,
artists, and
creatives...

and sometimes, i receive letters
from people
who write that
i've helped them
in some way,
that they've found
relation to my
poems, they've found
safety in my vulnerability...
and it brings a smile to my face,
because i know
that they know
that those poems written
so long ago
helped me too in some way,
and i know

that they know
that these letters have done
just the same
for me
today.

drought

overhead i saw the heron
gliding through the slate sky
as if it was nothing, but for me,
cemented to the ground,
it was everything.

i followed his descending trajectory and
had an approximation of his landing.

through thorns and ferns i ran, then
over dead leaves and exposed roots,
until i reached the green swamp
where our eyes locked.

for months it had been this way,
playing tag in the daytime shadows,
and when i'd approach he'd take flight,
but today was different.

"take the picture," the heron said.
"all right," i said, and i did.

he turned, exposing his backside,
and i did the same.

we walked away, never looking back.

i heard his feet crunching brush,

i felt my feet slip on the dead wet leaves.
he walks his path, i walk mine.
and that's the way it is,
now and forever.

my cat watches in silence

my cat watches in silence
as i pace midnight floors of agony
and trace shadows with stiff fingers
and lean against painted walls

my cat watches in silence
as i take post at the dirty window
and gaze at the ivory moon
and examine the validity of memories

my cat watches in silence
as i dance with madness and terror
and talk to ghosts unseen
and work through ideas not yet formed

my cat watches in silence
as i walk the dark hallways
and whisper words aloud
and begin to slow down

my cat watches in silence
and without judgment
and awaits the snap of my fingers
calling her to bed at last

the sun, the stars, the moon, and you

there are five park benches beneath twisted trees
and we choose the middle one.

we sit together staring forward into a cloud filled
future that was once untouched.

but now, here and between us,
between space and time,
parallel lives begin to fuse,
and are fragmented no more.

and somewhere in that library of
your mind, filed between
self-destruction and balancing peace,
i request that you please
pull out a filing card to
serve as a reminder:

as long as the lone heron
stands deep in the woods
on the brook-edge
and the egrets chase ghosts
of puzzle piece memory,
i am with you.

and for what it's worth,
in spite of all the tragedy

around us, please allow
me to say this, and perhaps
let it serve as a prayer:

thank you.

distress signal

the world seems darker tonight

there's not many cars on the highway
and the view from my window is blocked
by a dirty screen that needs a good cleaning

the world seems darker tonight

i filled the new bird feeder with seed
wondering what birds it might
bring tomorrow morning

the world seems darker tonight

outside i left my porch light on
the last attempt at a distress signal
that will again go unnoticed

the world seems darker tonight.

on the eve of my 30th birthday

people need distractions.
they crave and
seek distractions.

they find any way
to shift their thoughtless
thoughts from their
unfulfilled lives they believe
they are fulfilling
and settle for anything
other than what is
before them.

any distraction.
by any means.
anything at all.

i on the other hand
stand inside the darkness
of the house i grew up in
on the eve of my 30th birthday
and look out from the window
upon the bird feeders in the rain
and begin to weep
as no birds eat the seed
and the sun still shines.

the night after my 30th birthday

i walked in
and both
bartenders
said, "hi tohm."
"hello," i said
and before i took
a seat
the glass was
full and
awaiting
placement.
i thanked them both
and they said,
"you're welcome."
after i sat down
i asked for
the menu
i was hungry
and the night
was young.

eight years of filth

cleaning
eight years of
filth from the car floor,
dashboard, windows,
and rearview mirror
with cleaning wipes
that indicate:
'no residue or crud left behind'

i find it parallels my marriage—
however, in both cases
the wipes lied.

Christmas 2020

kaydence woke first then shook dylan awake—
with bloodshot eyes i watched it all
through the baby monitor

the clock read 6:14am

stampeding feet rattled my room
"daddy daddy it's christmas!" kaydence screamed
"it's too dark out" i said
"that's how you like it" dylan said

i sighed, "gimme ten minutes"

they crawled into my bed,
kicked my spine a few times
and burrowed their cold feet
beneath my ribs.

an hour later i awoke
the clock read 7:14am

"all right, all right" i said "just fifteen more minutes"

fifteen minutes later i was out of bed first,
stretching and cursing the gods
who blessed me with such
beautiful creatures

slowly we went downstairs,
the sun was up and
we had presents to open

7/11 poem

over at the 7/11 on main street,
i check in with the local clerk
who often tells me his thoughts
on the world at large

he's a strange guy, not bad,
just odd, and someday he'll
be locked away with me

but today he tells me,
"i do not like this,"
and points to his mask

i tell him, "i know man, it sucks,
but what can you do?"

"it very sucks man, it very sucks"

i smile but he can't see it

i walk to the register,
pay a different clerk,
leave the store and
dream of better days.

i sat and sat and sat and sat

i sat in a parking lot
and watched the sun set
behind a bunch of trees
as people drove home in cars
they couldn't afford,
sparrows flew back to their nests,
and gnats and moths
buzzed around my car…

and i sat
and sat
and sat
and sat

avoiding nothing but going home
for no reason other than
not wanting to be home;
i left the cat extra food,
filled the water dish,
and scooped the litter box,
it was all taken care of…

so i sat
and sat
and sat
and sat

while the sun continued dipping
down behind the trees,
casting salmon streaks
through the disappearing sky,
pinching clouds into orange smoke …

and i sat
and sat
and sat
and sat

eventually knowing i'd go home,
change into my house shorts,
pet the cat,
lift some weights,
rub my head,
drink some beer,
fill the bird feeders,
and scratch my ass…

but i sat
and sat
and sat
and sat

mustering the courage to take
all the thoughts out of my head,
hoping maybe one good poem
would be found amongst the river
of shit pouring out…

but i sat
and sat
and sat
and sat

watching the sun disappear
beneath the town's skyline,
feeling the new jersey air
grow cooler and colder,
finally ready to go home.

Tohm Bakelas is a social worker in a psychiatric hospital. He was born in New Jersey, resides there, and will die there. His poems have appeared in numerous journals, zines, and online publications. He is the author of 13 chapbooks, one full length book of poetry, and his work has been nominated several times for the Pushcart Prize. He runs Between Shadows Press.

Other Titles by Tohm Bakelas:

Orphan Crows (Analog Submission Press, 2018)

Destroy My Wound (Budget Press, 2018)

In Living Rooms (Iron Lung Press, 2018)

Decaying Sun Under Noontime Rain

(Analog Submission Press, 2019)

(UnCollected Press, July 2019)

Vacation Poems (Medusa Publishing Press, 2019)

No Place To Be (Holy&intoxicated Publications, 2019)

Cheap Booze and Shitty Poems

(Analog Submission Press, 2020)

Even the Spiders are Despondent (death of workers

whilst building skyscrapers, 2020)

Punk Poets are Pretentious Assholes

(Between Shadows Press, 2021)

Under The Same Moon (Between Shadows Press, 2021)

Flexeril Haikus (Between Shadows Press, 2021)

Stare Into The Sun (Between Shadows Press, 2021)

Three Poets 5 (Hicka Thrift Press, 2021)

BLACK DRAGON POETRY SOCIETY
CERTIFIED AND APPROVED